TRANSFORMATIVE BELIEFS: COUNTERBALANCE

Ihsan Jones

Copyright 2018

All Rights Reserved

ISBN 978-0-9985131-5-7

Dedication

This book is dedicated to my children. You are my source of sunshine and inspiration.

CONTENTS

Prologue 2

    IMBALANCE ii

Chapter 1-SPECTRUM 1

    Debugging the myths that we can't withstand the pressure of our wants and desires: 3

    A Leaders Influence 5

    Our Own Power 6

    -The Power of Influence- 9

Chapter 2-The Conquest of Virtues 15

    -Confidence Building- 15

Chapter 3-Deduction & Reasoning: The Super Power of Prowess 27

Chapter 4- Pragmatic Placement 37

Chapter 5- Repeating Souls 43

Chapter 6- Randomness... 49

-INTERIM- 60

    About the Super visits… 66

    Emotions Run High 69

Chapter 7- All the Things That Matter.. 72

    The Concept of Nothingness 74

    The Structure of Imbalance 77

Conclusion 80

Counter-Balance.. 81

    Displacement/Replacement/Virtual Souls... 84

Ihsan Jones

Ihsan Jones

PROLOGUE

We can work on ways to continually improve our conduct. Much of it has to do with channelling the synergies surrounding our wisdom, beliefs, and conduct. We can take charge based on our deepest connections to our inner-most and truest feelings.

God gave us feelings so that we could: show them, communicate, develop a sense of belonging and self-worth. It is how people of all faiths and backgrounds have communicated throughout the centuries. It all comes from our "gut" reaction, whether it is a 'belly laugh', a smile, tears, or any other sentiment that we can express since we have a range that carries a whole host of them. I call that range- a scale. A scale along the spectrum where sentiments are drummed up and played as tunes that keep us in alignment with what God wants us to do-which is to initiate our self-control. Everything is based on and rooted in how we respond- to be good at and successful at honing and channeling the senses.

The criteria for success, is not how the body responds, but what we do with those responses AFTER the initial reaction. Head-weights are an effective tool-that we talk about later in this book. Meanwhile, what's addressed, is the autonomous response mechanism that guides us.

We are guided by our inner vision. That vision includes how we might feel-but also our values-which is the 'weighted' response. Somethings can become more- "heavy" based on your opinions.

A weighted-response, is similar, to a measured response (that inner vision), however, there are practical ways of thinking in which to guide us. We can use the spectrum as we are guided along the scales. This way, we can present a more balanced approach to effectively use the tools as measures of our success. Thus, effectively, measuring and gaging the way we feel. OK, realistically, a lot of things can't be controlled. Senses can run amok. And like the blind leading the blind, you can become 'victim' to your autonomous responses. It is like being held hostage in a situation that you didn't intend or anticipate being in.

Ihsan Jones

There's an array of responses that we have. But it is not only the autonomous responses that I am concentrating on that mostly involve the senses. This book dives deeper into an exploration of attitudes and patterns that develop overtime that can and will get us into trouble- when not checked. There is a host of ways to "offset" these attitudes and sentiments that can put us in precarious situations; but can also be our saviors. The purpose of this book is to develop a deeper understanding of what those tools are and how we can effectively, channel them.

Counterbalance is a way of reflecting on the constraints we have regarding our faith in being who we want to be.

It is a way to secure a lifetime of meaningful interactions and engagement that's meant to make our deposits in life more meaningful.

We can better ourselves in an elegant way by dispensing with vices- that make us co-dependent. We can co-op our future by reflecting on our past in such a way that engagement in life and with human beings is more meaningful.

Unmeaningful things that we do are seemingly bland. Unmeaningful, does not mean insignificant, but it can be considered bland at best, for not having a bang or impact. They're caught in the middle of

TRANSFORMATIVE BELIEFS: COUNTERBALANCE

the spectrum where they could become lively again depending on what we do.

Futures are determined by past mistakes but it's our life's fortitude that gets us through. We can be going through something and not completely understand how we ended up in a situation. Many situations are beyond our reach, and out of control-but many are not.

For example: an interaction, no matter what kind, requires some sort of engagement. Basically, an action will elicit a reaction. What reaction is debatable-which is the part that we address here. This book deals with techniques that can be highly effective at countering what is called intuitive response.

Intuitive response is our gut feeling- or initial reaction, whether its displayed or not.

How do your feelings rank among the spectrum? Some can be more prominent than others depending on our personalities. There are complex reasons for intuitive response- such as which zodiac sign you fall under or even how you've felt about something similar in the past. This is the reason why, and how we believe we can apply the antidotes. Because the spectrum does not change-only our behavior and our responses do.

Ihsan Jones

It's a matter of recall that's facilitated by past performance. Past performance whether remembered or not as it has registered on the brain, will be our greatest ally or foe. If we look at the power of deduction and reasoning, we are being seduced into a state of consciousness that makes us aware of past behavior under similar circumstances. Our reaction time is controlled by timing and the sting or bite of the situation. We are being seduced into a sentimental passageway that lays clear the path and based on which sentiment is awakened- we will be emotionally controlled. Breaking through the barriers has to do with the powers that channel the senses. Some will become more robust while other sentiments, or the way you feel about something, will fade. Life becomes a process of seduction and reasoning based on what we have deduced from the predicament. We are seduced into how we feel. Precarious as it may sound, the exact problem that we must face regarding our sentiments, the alignment along the scale- becomes prominent. It is front and center and more pronounced because the sliding scale will grasp whatever appeals to it at the time.

TRANSFORMATIVE BELIEFS: COUNTERBALANCE

BUT we can REPEL anything that is not in alignment with our Values, Vision, and Beliefs. This is what God wants us to do. To filter out the various things-through our sentiments, with restraints.

In a sense, because of our similar qualities that are aligned on the spectrum such as sentiments that are strummed up…we basically, give what we get. But we also can do a takeaway of many of the things we don't need or will never use. That is why the consciousness stream measures the rise of the tide so -to -speak when it comes to how much or how far we are aroused. We are repeating souls.

Meaning, that whatever we can feel on a particular- day, we can also feel on another. The sentiments will rise with the tide but the avenue for adjusting them remains constant. The scales are measured along the spectrum as nothing at first since no response has been required. But then it develops as it is stroked and stoked by the realization of your displacement (whether you are at ease or not). This 'nothingness', or blandness as I call it, is from not knowing which sentiment to choose. It will be based on you having trained it. As we develop training of our conditional responses-which is like turning on a light switch-the host-which is our brain, will be interacting between our hearts and our minds.

An intuitive response would be to recall what we are used to doing. But we have the cognitive ability and ingenuity to change that display of behavior anytime we choose. It's what's called a "false sense of bravado" in many occasions which could possibly work to our advantage.

There is a certain amount of skill development and training that goes into "riding the tides" of the spectrum. Displaying an emotion is one thing -but getting rid of them altogether is another. We can rid ourselves of vices -and any mistakes we've made because of them. But getting rid of the sentiments associated with them or the knowledge that went into the development behind them, is another thing altogether. Essentially, we can't erase our past, but we can develop new strategies to take with us forward -into the future. Such as prowess, which we go into more detail about, in later chapters. Also, how to set up our own, what I call "virtual world", to counter any affects or residual side effects, that the spectrum leaves.

The imbalance represents a complete repertoire of what we can do to recreate "on stage" when we are 'acting'-in our virtual world. We must also pull out our armoire of trained and developed skills. This is all based on the influx of our instinct and raw emotions. This will also be how we can 'flip the scales' or what some deem as flipping the script. Before we break down the practical aspects of the spectrum, let's look at it on a higher level. This helps to put the spectrum into a wider context with a greater perspective. Although this book is about guiding you with pragmatic and sensible approaches about streaming consciousness that can help us arrive at sensible conclusions about who and what we are as related to our emotions and sensitivities. Thus, at a higher level, the spectrum also becomes more meaningful, if not yet practically, used.

For those that believe in God, most would agree that God is all seeing and all knowing. But there are some who question whether God exists. There is a dormant question amongst this group of folks with a consensus maybe that God is sleeping. And if God is sleeping, then why doesn't God arrive in time to save us from our woes and perils?

It may be because God doesn't have to govern our affairs consistently and constantly which would seem impossible. There are angels deployed on God's behalf that can take up that task. Why should God (our creator) have a hand in every issue we run across? Isn't this a well-oiled machine that can run on its own? Hasn't God already given us the tools and the wherewithal's to withstand the pressures-even as we feel that they are surmounting and can sometimes feel as if in a "pressure-cooker." Being under pressure doesn't necessarily mean under attack. It is a means of grabbing our attention so that we can use our sensibilities. We use our sensibilities as rational human beings and what's contained in our armoire, or chest. When someone talks about having something close to the bosom, it's true. It is our heart. Why do we think we have so many capabilities if, as they say- God, is sleeping? And, not always aware of the issues that we face?

God has given us a consciousness within our bodies that houses the mechanism that is used for governing our affairs. The angels are summoned at God's beckoning- to help prevent the chaos. We must essentially be saved. But we can also, save ourselves. Does that also make us Angels too? In a sense, we are also agents, under God's control and command. With implications that we can control our environment. Natures design and patterns are preset and a part of God's creation. We have an ability to save; but can also be saved in the process. And if God is sleeping…then God can rest peacefully, knowing that we (as consorts), are already set on a course that's under God's full control.

TRANSFORMATIVE BELIEFS: COUNTERBALANCE

The spectrum (on a larger scale), can be a whole host of things. But mostly, the spectrum is defined by the laws in which we live. Not the laws that we tend to create as we see fit. But the laws that are innate in all of us as a part -of mankind. In a convoluted sense, the spectrum is our entire makeup. Even as we are 'turned off', (resting or die) some remnants of our spectrum remain, momentarily. Until we can recharge.

Here's what the spectrum could look like-graphically:
*(reference pages in the back of book for the graphical drawing)

We have something in us that measures time, distance, and reaction. It's a display mechanism that has at the center of it-a spectrum. This system is unique to every individual. Not how it runs-because it's a well-oiled machine. But how it can display at any given moment.

A momentary reaction is a minute at best. But the real stars, present all the flavors, as the story unfolds. Something must manifest to make it real. Otherwise, it becomes fairytale like, or wishful thinking.

Our minds were made up the first time, when we gave our initial and gut reaction. But the mechanism has a control that starts from the heart, then ends with the brain. This is also why I said that it would need to travel the distance-because it knows its path. Blood rushes sequentially as our thoughts are captured randomly. We can pick up on lots of signals as they journey through the brain. The problem with stars bursting as if giving ignition-we don't always know -based on the spectrum-how our feelings will end.

It could be that the initial thought (course or pattern) was a pre-thought designed to get you awake (in the moment) and ready to start and rev up your engine. There are so many courses we could take, but it all ends up on the spectrum.

The spectrum is like a tick (clicking sound in your heart that goes-tick tock, tick tock, making the sound of a clock) and lies dormant until it is stoked. You can strum the strings to pull the pattern thus creating a hymn until it reaches where it will stop. This will be our initial reaction. This all happens so suddenly that it makes us wonder where we get our (instant) behavior. Behavior is automatic responses that are given when the path is traveled by the design agent that is stoked. The design agent can be anything that sets us off emotionally.

Picture it as wearing a cowbell and that every time we move-you could hear it. If we run, it clamors loud and fast like a heartbeat. But a slow methodical pull or twist in any direction, might not produce too much

TRANSFORMATIVE BELIEFS: COUNTERBALANCE

sound at all. Basically, that is how you get a reaction. It's based on the direction we are pulled. Sometimes the signal gets jammed when the cowbell is stuck-due to malfunctioning. Meaning we can get mixed signals resulting in mixed feelings.

A spectrum can be large or small depending on how big our heart is and the size of the brain since it is tied to it and needs to be examined. (this is a figurative translation for comparison but actual size- biologically, wouldn't matter). The spectrum is always the same however, because it houses the same ingredients which are, love, hate, jealousy, envy…etcetera. If we can name it…it's there.

Our cycles tick all the time but mostly they are at bay-like being docked, until they're agitated. Agitation is the key. The agitation of curiosity- leads to development of the brain. And when the brain receives this sort of stimuli it is developed from our autonomous pre-set behavior. It works like this…our hearts get stoked-the rhythm is picked up like a voice that is speaking to it-ALL this is happening inside the capsulized world that we call our body.

Much has been discovered about how the body works. It works on patterns as it picks up signals. But the mechanism, the one true mechanism-that rides the tides of time and stays the course-is a pre-set mode of original thought. Original thought is said to come from something that is outside of us, yet it is housed within. It's like the secret ingredient in a favorite recipe. No one knows what it is except the chef-but it sure is tasty. It's what makes the recipe original- its secret power punch called-a combination of ingredients but there's always that one special thing that enhances the rest. And for us when we're dealing with emotions and feelings-it's called the eyelids.

Eyelids are filters not screeners. They mostly will have to do a double take before they let something in. Am I really seeing this? Let's take a second look-just to be sure. Sometimes the vision is so long that our eyes will act as a scope and so the eyelids must shut in order to filter what it has captured. Once captured-the heart and then the mind take over.

None of this is part about how the eyelids work is phenomenal - there is much written about the biological functions, but what we don't know is the source. Examining any references to the source can get complicated because our brain powers pull is so strong that it spends most its time accepting and studying pre-thoughts.

TRANSFORMATIVE BELIEFS: COUNTERBALANCE

Pre-thoughts are designs of origination. They are ideas floating around that have already been there. But as a design, that would also mean that there is a pattern. The spectrum (as a pattern) would look something like this:

*(See an example drawing of the spectrum on last pages)

You would have to represent it as heat waves even though it was drummed up thought. Imagine cooking without knowing the ingredients. It would be a guessing game. That's how pre-thought originates. It is designed to essentially feed you. That is why with it, we have what's called- ingredients for life. We can't speculate where something (like a feeling) could land on the spectrum, because it first must be drawn out, put together, filtered, separated, then torn apart as a predesigned pattern with predestination towards the brains processing powers where it lands on the dot. The dot; is considered as the "dot of remembrance" because it understands everything that you took in before and therefor can shed significant light on what patterns have taken place over time with every emotive that you have taken in based on where it has landed on the spectrum. After some screening (brain power processing time)-which takes place very quickly; the screening can help give a measured and controlled response. But it is always feed- back that remains after the fact. That is, after the initial or original response that had already tapped into our emotions and landed somewhere on the spectrum. In other words, it is the brains screening skills that helps us to develop sentients from the patterns over time as we work to fine tune those responses. The dot (of remembrance) will be explained much more, later. The ordinance that's drawing from the realm of the spectrum is also depicted graphically so that you can visualize the mechanism in its course of action. Let's understand first and foremost, that we are being fed. Fed from pre-thoughts (as stimuli) that are designed to coincide with centers along the spectrum.

The spectrum represents a loud obnoxious awakening of our subconscious that can also be subtle. The subtleness is because sometimes we can't tell or feel that the spectrum is stirring our emotion until we're caught up in the heat of it. Like a rude awakening, our feelings are drawn towards the lines (waves and patterns) until they have landed. Our reaction time is tied to this as well. One example is that, if I'm pinched-I might feel it immediately depending on the force or, gravity. But if I'm punched - since I could also be knocked out-I would have to be consciously aware to respond. You can't do this sleeping. Sleeping can make you forgetful. I

TRANSFORMATIVE BELIEFS: COUNTERBALANCE

must be awake before I will become aware to react. The rhythm and patterns will work according to circumstance. Thus, a fleeting thought, that's grabbed, may not stick. I would have to be consciously aware to drive it to its destination which would be among the spectrum. So, it then shifts from the eyelids (what I have taken in), to the brain's reaction as a screener. Our reaction could be like the secret ingredients in a recipe, since we won't know what it is until we taste it. It could be sweet, sour or bitter.

Why is understanding the root cause so important? Because it leads to how we could control it.

Some people believe in forces. Forces are acts of nature that require us to react to a situation. We don't know what force we can pull out until we are faced with either-having to defend ourselves or to prove something. Force is never required for "lack of improvement". That would be an idle mind sitting at bay-waiting to be strummed or stoked-again.

If you can understand the spectrum and how it works, then you can muster up the controls that will handle anything that the world throws at you. In a quiet sense, you can become your own super hero. And why would you want to do that? Because being a super hero is the best that we can aspire to. So, we would need to muster up a feeling-that is controlled by our initial reaction, and after it has been filtered and screened (for control purposes) by our brain in order to master it.

This is the inclination we have for working with the tools. The tools are plenty-but I'd say that the main tools we need, are spiritual. If we have stirred our soul-then we've stirred our spirit. And God is in control of that. It all goes back to that one favorite and often- times illusive ingredient, with the underlying principle…

That which we give-we may not get back.

That which we take-can also be taken from us.

Another way to say it, is that along the spectrum of our inner solar cycle-judgements and purity are not synonymous. Judgements become the "outcome" of actions -when possibly it wasn't the aim. So, it is by default, what we end up with. It may not have been the goal-but as a result-it has become the end game. We clear our consciousness only by cleaning up or actions. Even if you have cleaned up your act by saying, "I didn't intend for this or for that to happen" the results are the same, if anywhere on the spectrum-your categories of enamorment are crossed. That's when you won't be able to make the distinction between good (intent) vs the greater

TRANSFORMATIVE BELIEFS: COUNTERBALANCE

(good). You could be feeling a certain way and trying to mask it. Which could be your greatest influence.

Here are techniques for getting rid of:

Jealousy...etc.

Well, it may not get rid of it (the sentiment) entirely, but when it does crop up, you can refer to this assortment of counter- intuitive measures that would be based on the reasons for your sentiment:

Is it because of beauty, looks, strength, wealth, status...?

You can counterbalance any part of substance -as a conquest- starting with yourself. Waging a war (internally) as if it were, in context- a contest to be won. The contest would be to win against- that which you are fighting.

TRANSFORMATIVE BELIEFS: COUNTERBALANCE

An Introduction to Imbalance

"Your raw, "gut" reaction; is your true self.

But it does not have to be your lasting impression".

IJ

IMBALANCE

As our consciousness awakens…Is God Sleeping?

In a larger sense, the Spectrum is…

It can be depicted as a diagram involving every emotion and sentiment that we have. This is what I call our; "Enamored- Faith".

We are 'smitten' by the things that we are capable of. When 'smitten', we become truly enamored, which is a combination of "love and awe". In the spirit of faith-about the things in which we can do-we believe that everything is possible. And when I say-everything, I mean, the good, the bad, and everything in between. It is infectious in all of us- to become enamored. Even with self-doubt, we know that we still are capable.

But the spectrum doesn't just represent possibilities. The spectrum represents-what is. With all things possible-God can sleep soundly and without worry about the world and its turmoil. If you want proof; Everything has an order and sits on its axis as it turns. As acting agents

TRANSFORMATIVE BELIEFS: COUNTERBALANCE

(from heaven), we deploy the skills that the mechanism has chosen for our battles. Our duties are fulfilled by pre-conditions, and everything along the spectrum has implications.

In a sense, living is a pre-programmed condition that surpasses our faith in anything that we could believe. It also coincides with our- enamor about faith and what that implies. In our living quarters, (here on earth), it is divided among earth and various other spacious planetary atmospheres. We survive because of waste and opportunity go hand in hand. Waste is the byproduct of living and becomes an essential part of how we survive. Waste becomes reconstituted as opportunities. It's called matter, because everything should and/or something should always matter to us in our minds. That's how we should see it. That life has a substance. We can be rejuvenated as pre-programmed substance. The substance can be turned off or on by the spectrum. Sometimes we lie dormant or in between which we would consider as nothing or bland- before we are ignited again. Bland is a rotational spirit that preexists as a condition. It means that everything is held at bay until a consciousness is aroused and a decision has been made about our arrival. This internal fortitude is as a time clock that proves beyond measure that we are resilient and can face anything. If we look at the spectrum as a waveband with channels flowing through our bodies, that could be a more accurate depiction. But graphically, all our emotions can be charted because we have felt them in some sort of way. Thus, sentiments become our dominant argument when it comes to presentation along the spectrum. Our spectrum is bland or humdrum when we are at peace. We feel neither highs nor lows about almost everything until something becomes allocated into a slot. But as we are turned on, or tuned up I should say, we are affected. There also can be cross wires in our paths that doesn't know which way to go because of sentiments. That's why we should be grounded in our faith (principles) to see our way through the array of crossed signals. Everyone knows what happens when wires get crossed. Essentially, there can be "mixed" signals wreaking havoc among the spectrum.

That is why honing the skills and using the tools talked about in this book can work wonders.

As a tool, I've gained insight through intra-gleaning. Intra-gleaning is a concept and has become one of my greatest tools. Intra-gleaning is a combination of using both spirituality as a guide to maintain a sense of morality, but also to remain human. If becoming a better human being is not what we seek, then we would find our place amongst the ranks of animals. Many come with a separate set of emotions. They are desperate and become anxious according to how they would feel. And you cannot predict if they will separate their emotions from their entire actions. Humans are different. We are not only capable of 'masking' or hiding our true emotions, but we can separate feelings based on our course of interaction. Animals will do almost anything to survive. I'm not saying that we won't. I'm just saying that our sense of judgment is what tends to separate us. It's hard to predict an animal's behavior, but even more-so; humans. Humans are faced with all- possibilities, both good and bad.

Having "Enamored faith – means believing in our greatest strengths as our allies and using them as tools that can and will keep us in the wings of prayer and truth as we become closer to God.

Ihsan Jones

TRANSFORMATIVE BELIEFS: COUNTERBALANCE

CHAPTER 1-SPECTRUM

Behavior-develops with a pattern

There are Forces

Knowing these two things can set you free. You can live free as a bird soaring high. The main ingredient is that God is at the origin of where we can produce original thought. Most of it is pre-set, as things are filtered from our hearts to our minds. And while God, may be the main ingredient-the secret to the success of the main ingredient remains elusive-until we can figure it out. I'm one to admit, that hearing lots of stories about God and what God can do-I'm truly a believer in that concept of origination with God at the helm and us as a part of the source.

Ihsan Jones

God uses us to complete the main ingredients. God does this by feeding us with righteousness. A righteousness that is everlasting. When we are promised "bliss" as in ascendance to heaven after living on earth - according to scripture, we are also told that we will continue to succeed our predecessors. This was to be WITHOUT purpose. There was no clause on our being here except to live. If we were given purpose ahead of time, we might not be living our own lives. Therefore, we live as if we are under a pressure cooker- subject to our feelings but also knowing that God is at the helm.

We can effectively control who we are and who we can become by exploring the changes that take place within our bodies.

The spectrum is about knowing the sentiments that arise with our impulses. Then, eliciting behavior that can counteract -those initial effects. Harm can be done when there is no reconciliation or correction.

Correction of any impulsive responses involve direction-like direction in a play; what it is you want to feel, not, what it is that you do feel. It would be how you would want the narrative perceived.

TRANSFORMATIVE BELIEFS: COUNTERBALANCE

It's called reflection. Reflection along the spectrum not only helps us understand it better but gives us some tools to use as measures.

DEBUGGING THE MYTHS THAT WE CAN'T WITHSTAND THE PRESSURE OF OUR WANTS AND DESIRES:

This is a depiction of our inner solar cycle (*see drawing on last pages*) that is an interpretation of our inner and intimate feelings and how they would flow.

Some categories will overlap depending on perspectives.

You can fuse two things together without confusing the concept-all you would need to do to debug it, is to -not falsify how you really feel.

If you can honestly say that one thing belongs in a particular- category, then it will be easier to address our feelings.

Ihsan Jones

I had experienced at a young age most, if not all, of these:

- Jealousy
- Seclusion
- Isolation
- Separation

   *(you can add others to this list)

Add anything that has an "ism", such as racism, fascism, separatism, etc. You name it! I've likely experienced it in my lifetime leading up until now. At the very least, I've heard of it and understand what it stands for. These things will fit into our reality in some way to influence how we feel. And not necessarily by how much we've been led to believe by leaders that have influence. Respectively, we should all work on the sentiments elicited by these.

TRANSFORMATIVE BELIEFS: COUNTERBALANCE

A LEADERS INFLUENCE

Many leaders will buy into the concept of the greater good. And if a leader's aim and goal is to do good, with their influence, then they can do a lot of good. But if it's bad, disastrous things can happen. Therefore, it all leads back to Purpose-which some refer to as Intent.

I refuse to believe that the "intent" is more important than the outcome. More, or less, when an act or deed is committed, it can be judged by its consequences-then the intent-gets lost in the fray.

What good is intention if it has resulted in catastrophe?

I also don't believe in sacrificing (souls) for what is called the "greater good". Who's greater good would that be? Mankind? Or, our own selfish agenda based on our limited insight and perspective. I'm not here to judge someone's eyesight as faltering. I'm discussing it in the greater context of applying "keen" eyesight. The greater good is not necessarily for the sacrifice of souls. The greater good, for all practical purposes, should be for the benefit of mankind. No one should have to suffer as the result of someone's else's inclination towards the so-called-greater good. Even in times of wars-we should use our greatest restraints.

1. Can you walk in the other persons shoes?
2. Understanding that there is always more to the puzzle-meaning that no one is perfect even if (in your eyes) they would appear that way

Also, for the time being, as you experience your own "transference of indifference" into your own virtual reality-make sure that you are grounded, and your feet are planted so that you can come back from dreaming in the clouds. This can help you face or conquer your demons. Let those thoughts float away along with that dream until it dissipates. Only then, can you move on to face another storm to conquer what might be simmering in the background waiting to brew.

OUR OWN POWER

The consequences of not recognizing your own power is that you could be destroyed in the process. You could be destroyed if you get defaced by the rapture of, say…jealousy (as a sentiment example) …etc.

TRANSFORMATIVE BELIEFS: COUNTERBALANCE

But you could also turn the thought associated with those destructive tendencies around to work to your advantage.

That doesn't mean you will develop a false sense of bravado-it means that you are determined to win. To win, over and above what those destructive feelings could ever make you do. You can develop tunnel vision from the destructive feelings if the pull is strong. Then you will be traveling down a dark path like a force of wind stirring up and impacting everything along the way. You need helpers. People or friends that could now become as servants-to help you in delivering your results which are to -come out on top – since you are feeling inadequate or short changed.

Go into your virtual reality world-pick and choose some virtues to work on. Some that will stick. Use it as part of a plan to help conquer the fear (the emotive) of what's captured between our hearts and mind. The thoughts of you wearing the crown (in your dreamland) will not escape you. You must win. You have a direct influence over the outcome, not initially, as demonstrated by our first reaction-but intuitively, as you plan to give a structured response.

Ihsan Jones

The virtue that you choose -if it is counter intuitive-will help lessen or get rid of the feeling altogether, that carry those destructive thoughts that you might have.

Everything is not about conquering the enemy (that which you feel is better (than you)) as you have already spoken your inferior thoughts into existence. But it would be based on your judgements about the situation after gaining insight. Therefore, you would need to (literally) walk (those thoughts) back-by establishing virtues-of counterbalance.

Highlight the virtue-tell yourself that you too are (beautiful (in your own way) as defined by -you. Always remember that beauty is in the eyes of the beholder and that the beauty that you see-can also be in yourself- (even if through your virtual reality world), if you choose to do it.

But if you need to be judged by those same beauty standards from others (that surround you)-it won't work. You can only compete with your placid beauty with others is a placebo.

The placebo effect would work on others only if they are enamored or snared (temporarily) under your influence as an effect. After the placebo (effect) wears off-which would not have worked on everyone, (they may have just been too afraid to stand up to you and pretended to follow along); it would all be based on your power.

-THE POWER OF INFLUENCE-

We maybe can win (to soothe our ego). But we really haven't won because like the windstorm created in the tunnel-you also would be caught up by your own visions-thus creating a version of the person who would be looking in the mirror uttering the infamous words like snow white- "who's the most…attractive…beautiful…famous.., etc. (you fill in the blanks)

Therefore, an intuitive counterbalance is needed from your armoire, or chest. You can turn the wheel-see which counter balance that could be.

*(see drawing of wheel of counterbalance in back pages of book)

Its best to focus on the virtue. Being that it is virtual -it can soon become your reality as you begin to juxtapose to switch positions.

You can also be caught up in a snare. That would mean that you have fed into the remnants of the trap of (*jealousy* for example) long enough to be pulled sideways in order to throw you into some dirt. You can't have it both ways-throwing salt, then trying to make it sweet again. Just simply use the remedies that are most effective.

God gave us our intuitive power to go along with our feelings. It's not that there is anything wrong with the feelings that we have but it is to keep them in check. Our visions are what makes us either stronger or weaker in the pull of things. Like a snare or snag, we can get caught up. When that happens its best to act fast. Use the remedies at your disposal-which would be your virtues. These are virtues you have developed or either acquired. The compass map has the virtues listed and those that can be used as counterbalance.

Do some deep breathing exercises to let the air out. A sigh of relief is felt when all the anxiety that was felt as a bite or sting has left.

Example- you can be beautiful -in your own right…in your own way.

But if you truly are jealous-even temporarily-then use the virtue compass as an intuitive guide to counterbalance and help you even out the path from the tunnel you are starting to cross. This way, a wind storm can't brew and there won't be casualties of war left as a result, (such as -loss of

TRANSFORMATIVE BELIEFS: COUNTERBALANCE

friends, etc.) from people being influenced and choosing sides-based on your interactions.

You can essentially end up boosting folks to work against or for you based on your warped sense of reality.

For example, if the people (in your circle) are drawn to beauty-it's likely that you are too. And if you feed it with negative energy-it will get stronger. And you will become isolated by choosing sides with only those that think like you (to boost your own ego). Basically, those who might also be jealous or by the way of influence, have been made to be jealous.

Using jealousy as our example, is an easy one. Most of us have felt that way and none of us can avoid that feeling because it's a natural part of our makeup. It can become excitable in us- that's when it becomes a problem and we would have to execute a plan.

-Excitable Behavior-

This is when it (an emotive) is fed. It is fed by either attraction or deflection. It can be attracted both negatively and positively along the scale. It is said that you can "reap what you sow". But envy only sees one outcome-that's why it's called tunnel vision. That outcome could be like the mirror said; if you wanted to influence it to not give an honest answer, by saying -that "you are the most beautiful...etc." (again, snow white analogy).

Let the virtual reality wheel answer this for you. Build yourself up with self-esteem, to help your false sense of identity and pride have a safe landing. Use an alternate (ego) boosting technique to help you see that you too can become as beautiful, powerful, or whatever it is that you want to be. Just be sure to make it last long enough-well, so that you will experience it long enough-in your virtual reality world-that you won't have a need for destructive thoughts that seek to destroy anyone or anything afterwards; nor do something that would want to make others rally to your cause- which would be giving you false impressions by praising you as the most (beautiful) etc. even when not true-echoing back the mirrored response.

Beauty will continue to be in the eye of the beholder, and people will have hidden agendas that may fulfill their self-aggrandized requests.

Put a positive spin on the situation because your initial reaction had already surfaced and led you to think negatively (to place yourself as inferior) - otherwise you would have let that feeling of jealousy that cropped up - remain a fleeting thought.

TRANSFORMATIVE BELIEFS: COUNTERBALANCE

It would have dissipated pretty- fast, if you hadn't fed it.

That doesn't mean that the thing you see as a "foe"- (beauty, power, etc.) goes away. It just means that it goes away as being your own (self-made) crisis of competition.

If you happen to like the same beauty standards that your object of attention has -then you can adopt them too, realizing that- on you-they may not have the same results but that- it is OK- to aspire to the same kind of beauty when you admire it.

But virtual realities can do wonders-especially when you are using the counterbalance spectrum tools.

It's not always our 'feelings' about things that can be wrong-but there is also the fact that others can hurt you. While this book concentrates on the "tools" to help us master our destiny and chart our course as far as 'controlling' our feelings, what about those things that are outside of our control? Where does the counter (intuitive) balance come in? It doesn't. But that's OK. In a lot of instances, when you are the target of someone else's aggression, deception or schemes, oftentimes that wrath is unavoidable. In those cases-not even the virtual reality wheel would apply. Not until after the fact, anyway. In most of those cases-you will have to react in the moment. And depending on whether your virtue closet (armoire) is full, determines how you will react. Who's to say what's right or wrong in the situation when you are defending yourself? Your first reaction is probably the most important. But it may not be your last. it depends on the crime (perceived or not) that would determine what level your feelings have risen too.

Will there be turbulence? Most likely. Can the situation end up with bad feelings where it seems as if it cannot be turned around? That's a possibility.

We may become enamored by our feelings about a situation or things -but when we feel aggrieved, we will most likely -react in the moment. And no amount of values or virtues can help you in that situation unless you are strong enough (at the time of the occurrence or scene of the crime) to remember them. Thinking about the greater good just might apply in this situation.

CHAPTER 2-THE CONQUEST OF VIRTUES

Intra-gleaning: intra spiritual guidance and reflection

Here are tools:

-CONFIDENCE BUILDING-

One tool from the armoire or chest is to engage in confidence building exercises. These are exercises that can build self-esteem. You need self-esteem to be aware of who you are and what you can become. A self-awareness assessment starts like this:

Ihsan Jones

Do I often feel ashamed?

Am I ashamed of myself?

Do I walk with confidence?

Etc.

Esteem building starts young. It is one of those things we need in our earliest foundation. Children and babies need it, but adults do too.

We should- always be engaging in confidence building workshops to learn techniques that can keep our self- esteem beaming.

Building self-esteem is a powerful way to help with your determination to spin the wheel to find the virtues that are best in all situations.

Look to self-esteem as a way of making you not feel guilty about your initial thought of jealousy etc., because having the confidence that can overcome them by using counter intuitive virtues is powerful, itself.

You can walk with more pride and having confidence in self-esteem that has been built up and is rooted in cleansing out the evil-pre-thoughts that we have that can lead to our elusive feelings (running amok).

There are some strong explorations in our feelings, but most of it has to do with the heart.

TRANSFORMATIVE BELIEFS: COUNTERBALANCE

When we are enamored with something

(struck, smitten, hold in high esteem)

There is a fondness. The fondness of many things is buried deep inside the soul. Many people that hold spiritual beliefs (and some that don't), also feel that the key to understanding the soul is buried in the heart- and not necessarily the mind. Although connected, sentiments that are filtered through the heart are also being screened by the brain. As a counterintuitive effect, the brain can handle almost anything that's dumped there. But it is our virtues that are called upon to do much of the screening. The virtues that we have or hold near and dear will also bear out as our truths.

Speaking of truths; from a spiritual perspective, the heart and brain should be in unison. We are supposed to have feelings that can unleash or release the trapped soul. Spiritual guidance is important enough to help us understand the cause and effect of this relationship. If I have sinned, I would need to do soul searching. Somewhere, buried in the heart perhaps, are feelings about certain things. If my brain screens using screening powers- I can easily be persuaded to think a certain way. Perspectives are a part of the screening process that must occur from things that have been dumped in the brain.

[A soul's spiritual quest is to make use of its virtues]

We can scream all day about what we want and need. But at the end of the day-a powerful force-that's known and associated with our feelings -called sentiment- will have to emerge. Regardless of how our sentiments are persuaded-this inter-exploration of our hearts is essential for our well-being. We eventually would have to make a judgement call as to not only what it is that we really want-but more importantly, what we're going to do?

Some will use the 'greater good scenario' I gave earlier-where it is that your intentions matter but regardless of consequences, there might be casualties of war. What they could be blurring out, is that this could also be viewed as "sacrifice"; the sacrifice of souls that in this instance won't matter because they have deemed it as such.

In other words, the heart that is tied to sentiments-doesn't always win. The heart in its pure state-wants you to 'feel' everything so that you can weigh and judge the consequences of your actions that are tied to the decision.

That's why it lets you "feel" it-full force, first. Then the brain steps in and asks, "wait a minute-have we encountered this situation before?" What did we do? What should we do? Thus…its screening.

A Graphical Representation

The flow of electrical signals can be viewed as 'impulses of correspondence' rapidly darting throughout the body. Mostly, they stay on course. *(see back pages)

There is a 'dot' of remembrance that we each have. This dot represents 'the point of inclusion' and will respond and react as impulses are sent.

We are wired in such a way that we have memory modules on spectrums. A screening process in motion in the brain shuffles through them in order to trigger a response.

First, there is the rapid response-like an emergency responder, it is the initial order that the path will take. Second, we have what's called a 'gut reaction'. It's the outside stimuli that recognizes this force. Third, we have what I call -shutter and twitch. Shutter/twitch; is the switching mechanism that shifts throughout the brain and that can be seen racing through the blood as spectrums that are pumped through our hearts. The rush and flow- of our feelings, our emotive feelings, are all wrapped up in this. And can be caught in a current of ungratefulness, and ingratitude. The switching is done so that we can control it. But the initial 'gut' response that overflows from the blood rush, must be felt first before anything else kicks in.

This is where you will find that a treasure chest of values come in. If it is full- you will have many to choose from.

Treasure chests (our armoires)- are thoughts that are built up around the sentiments we carry about certain, things. The memory can give the rapid response for only an instance, but it can last a lifetime. We are filled with values from heaven, and that is what makes up our SOUL.

Those values don't lie, and cannot be changed, but they can react differently among the spectrum.

The enemy in most of us-is the enemy or causation in all of us. It is the ability to use the spectrum in such a way that it will seek balance. Balance is an opportunity for the signal to lay, rest, reclaim, or remain at bay.

It is a powerful experience that takes place unconsciously, but our hearts and mind know it.

TRANSFORMATIVE BELIEFS: COUNTERBALANCE

--It is the pieces of us that make up our energy-that we can expend and expel.

Arising throughout the course is our raw, unadulterated, uncut, unfiltered-feelings that show us who we are and what we're made of.

It is an agreement that the alignment with nature is to give synonymous responses that are synchronized with earths patterns that can travel along a path-as a 'travel plan'-interacting with and escaping only death. These signals combatively-will live. This is where the 'dot' originates. At the twilight or twain-mark between life or death. An entry, and an exit, is known as a 'trigger' of our emotions, that are synchronized with our time clock. The time clock allows us to think clearly and separately about each, and every situation.

Responses don't lie. They are raw and uncut.

Our acting is a result of our screening capabilities. As we filter out that which we want to dispose of to regain our disposition.

We can try-again, as a mask-or cover-up to our first response or initial reaction.

The 'feelers' in our skin know how to make the impulses play out. The hair rises and falls with each semi-quasi response. Oil and sweat glands will rise to levels based on our control.

This is it in a nutshell *(see drawing in back pages of book). And although it doesn't necessarily include all the delicate intricacies that happen-it does provide us with the spectrum that shows us predictions (graphical representations) of how it can work.

*See the dot of remembrance Diagram in back pages of book
Explanations on the diagram:

There are two transactions taking place. One is the waves coming from the spectrum (where ever it would land) that go to what's called the dot of origin-that is like a memory dot. This memory dot or dot of remembrance is used as a filter or screener. It can detect whatever has gone on before to give a response back to the initial one to either neutralize its affects or embolden its spirit.

1. The inner "dot" of origin that makes the connection (drawing with larger circle and impulses

    surrounding the dot).

TRANSFORMATIVE BELIEFS: COUNTERBALANCE

2. (An Arrow pointing to) the secret dot of remembrance on the diagram

   The secret dot of remembrance can be reached only through passageway. The passageway is the electrical impulses that are sent throughout the brain after passing from the heart. The membranes are sealed and locked (larger outer circle) so that nothing escapes or gets out except through the passageway.

3. The picture depicts bodies of passage in equilibrium and directional flow (as impulses). They are like diamonds pivoting in rough sand that must be filtered constantly to show their brilliance.

Development takes place in the 'womb' of our brains. That is where we are shaped and formed. The biological clock tells us that we will only have a certain amount, of signals that can be sent as impulses throughout our life, therefor our life is finite. But the soul can infinitely send these signals long after the body has collapsed/disintegrated.

On the graph:

The blood rushing cycle is a result of impulses known as 'feelers' - emotive attitudes. There is a pool of them constantly swimming around our blood used to connect. There is no single point of origin-as long as it makes it through the membrane (to the dot) the pulse is recognized- an immediate response is given-then it must be screened for development. Development takes place in the brain. At the dot of origin- pulsations come from the heart (from along the spectrum) then proceeds to the brain, to make a direct connect, from the blood that's rushing through it. (A sperm and egg can be a similar example, however, we are only talking about how 'feelers' connect on the spectrum). Electrical signals and impulses of 'correspondence' are rapidly darting throughout. They are designed to present the 'urge' or point of instigation. Because the signals can be capsulized and protected-each one or group of them can be considered 'flurries' of absent- thought floating in and waiting to be activated. What we have around us constantly is a life stream of currents.

As an outer stimulus-the thoughts and ideas are at bey waiting in the stream. As they would reach our spectrum (as emotions or feelers), they come back and forth as an exchange between the heart and brain. We can sometimes hear them – these outside flurries. But they belong

TRANSFORMATIVE BELIEFS: COUNTERBALANCE

to what we would call-entities. Which could also be ourselves (we're also angels).

There are scales of 'justice' along the spectrum. Not only can we equalize them, we can equate them to our consciousness and well-being. Then we become the pall-bearers for their arrival before and after our thoughts become buried. In the meantime-they can be masquerading around in the atmosphere as pre-thought.

Pre-thought is the mechanism that triggers recall. Impulses are our reaction to a situation. And 'thought' glands can glide their way as if they are 'heaven sent'.

Those are the messages. We can build from- them and upon- them. They can and do represent our characters throughout our long- lost generations.

We are a culmination of pre-thoughts of pre-messaging that takes place that is generated over time; and for us-may last a lifetime.

You will generate your pre-recorded responses to these messages to add to the fray.

Never think that there is a conclusion-just and end -result. That result is simply-how you will react.

Your reactions make up your living space that is housed in the spaces amongst the spectrum.

Your pulses and responses get sent constantly when they are housed in a body that can encapsulate them.

*　*　*

*note-This is a replica of my representation and it is spiritual. It is from my insight that has been gained as a result of ultra-gleaning. Ultra-gleaning provides a direct connection. A direct connection means-a way of associating with spirituality as aspects of the divine. Our bodies use pre-thoughts as waves and patterns of stimulus and suggestions. The inner spiritual realm is the body's temple and natural stimuli. It is the alkalinity to understanding our truths that can help us control who and what we are based on what we would want to be. Knowledge is not finite. But the spiritual realm houses the ways in which knowledge can set you free. (learn more about ultra- gleaning at the end of this book).

CHAPTER 3-DEDUCTION & REASONING: THE SUPER POWER OF PROWESS

Prowess is an art. [It is to have a skill or expertise in a particular-activity or field such as-e.g. bravery in battle]

The process of reasoning-deduces that prowess not only is a learned skill-but as a magic- art form, you have ability to apply it at random. Being adept at situational control means developing prowess from instinct. But another way to summon this spirit is when in dire-straights.

We all have the potential to stand up for something when it's usually about principle. Our virtues and values will dictate that to happen. However, prowess can be used even when you are lacking in judgement.

To apply reasoning is to be prudent and shrewd. That's what the screening process does (in the brain), it develops a sense of awareness about a particular- thing so that you rise to the occasion whenever there's a need. You can be soaring with ideas about something. But unless you can actually- use, the "best protocols" or applications, in a particular-circumstance, you can be spinning your wheels.

No worries. This is all a part of the journey into the learning process where prowess plays an important part. Honing skills for accuracy, is how you learn and mature.

Why is reasoning so important in our analogy about faith and how we can use the skills along the spectrum to get in touch with and control our feelings?

Because deductive reasoning is spiritual.

TRANSFORMATIVE BELIEFS: COUNTERBALANCE

Some would argue that it is the reasoning that gets you in the most trouble. I think that it is reasoning that can spare us from doing a lot of incompetent things. We can be learned (educated), we can be skilled. But it is our reasoning that can get us through the rough patches. Say, for instance, that you applied one of the techniques along the spectrum. Take jealousy for example. The best way to live, is to vicariously live through someone else. Even if it is momentarily. This is the best way of solving the puzzle of why you should ever be jealous in the first place. Regulating jealousy and reeling it in is an art. And this would take prowess.

Prowess is basically courage that you muster when faced with something that you need to handle.

It's courageous to begin the process of living as someone else. But that's exactly what you're doing when you dream about it. Automatic-displacement, puts you in the scene. Otherwise, why would you want it? We can want things for other folks and not be jealous of them. Experiencing automatic- displacement through this virtual world allows you intuitively to be safe where you would be able to say, "I can have these things too".

Usually, once the matter is deeply felt-with passion, sometimes you will no longer want it. At least not in the same capacity as you did initially. Much of it has dissipated-that feeling inside of wanting what others have that- elicits jealousy. Conjuring up the episode by displacement (placing yourself in the scene acting as if in someone else's shoes) can cause a reactionary effect whereby you either no longer need it (the object that you're being jealous of) or you will pursue it, but in a manner that it doesn't matter if someone else has it too. This would mean that your deepest thoughts are developed by stimulus from the atmosphere and anything that's outside of your domain (of control) can be reeled in -vicariously, if nothing else. Live as you want. As if you are escaping pride and judgment. That way, reasoning, as you can develop it-can never fail. That doesn't mean you won't have faulty reasoning. It just means that you are applying the filters exactly the way you want.

Your arsenal of tools (virtues and values) will be there to meet you as rapid response to our feelings that can get out of control.

TRANSFORMATIVE BELIEFS: COUNTERBALANCE

Some say that reasoning (when thinking too hard) about something can get you in lots of trouble. I believe it's the opposite. Although reasoning is seductive-it can give us the checks and balances we need because it is spiritually based. And no, it is not exactly what separates us from animals, because other animals, well, creatures, do think. What it does is help us to operate in a realm where we have a form of escape. That's our reality-and reasoning is your prowess on steroids. Our screeners are filters that develop in our brain to squeeze out the emotions that are coming from our heart. If you take this literally, you might not understand it at face value. But if you know that our brain power is used as a warning mechanism against all the vices we come across and/or run up against, whether random, selected, or otherwise. So, the purpose of having super powers is to show who we are and what we're made of/ although in the blink of an eye, even that can change.

The scale remains constant however, the spectrum or drum string, is the pattern by which we can fine tune until you at least get the rhythm right according to your heartfelt attachments.

Love is more than seductive prowess. It is reasoning unfiltered. Love can be our greatest form of escape (if we can live through it). But love has its faults and defaults-that's why we would use reasoning to regulate.

[There is no exact science when it comes to using the filters. The screeners are in place as protection and a shield for covering the heart.] Learn to conquer the demons and vices. All, of which-with added stimuli from the outside-remain inside.

Those vices you choose can be strummed to perfection. You will be on automatic pilot every time a sentiment arises. You can double check to see if your filters are in place so that your prowess can protect you. Live vicariously through others to see if the shoe fits. We will look through hind glass as a mirage in most situations. What if, will become the biggest question.

The tools that are developed along the spectrum are used to develop our prowess.

We can become skilled at something, but if that "something" takes over and consumes us (runs rampant in our thoughts-such as jealousy

TRANSFORMATIVE BELIEFS: COUNTERBALANCE

etc., then we would need the checks and balances of the filters-which are designed as our deductive reasoning.

There's a border crossing at the tentacles of success, and failure-and prowess is in the middle of it.

Understand your limits-the power (of deductive reasoning) that you possess. But most of all, know that your prowess-which is a superpower-can get you through almost anything.

The spectrum explained in more detail... (see diagrams in back pages)

1. Name the feeling (emotion)
2. Name the symptom of that feeling

    Example: (when it is pulled in either direction. When it is inflated)

Then describe - Is it an infatuation that you're feeling or the real deal?

Is this image (that I admire, or don't like), a mirror image or a mirage?

If, a mirage, it can dissipate as I've lived vicariously through it.

But if as a mirror-that can be inescapable since it reflects- back whatever I feel, see, and/or want to do.

Ihsan Jones

Maybe it's meant to be the image that's kept. Maybe…just maybe, as I daydream about it and wish -with all my heart- the image can become a permanent fixture. Which won't be me living vicariously through it any more to satisfy my wants and needs. It was just a simulation of what's to come. As I gather all my thoughts and collectively put in the skills-or prowess that's needed to accomplish this feat. Then, even if it's felt along the spectrum-which gives rise to highs and lows (about the situation) until it is fine tuned. I can turn this pretend or make believe into reality.

This is what we do, all the time.

The spectrum of knowledge and consciousness is there. It is the filters that apply screening that is strummed up through emotions.

With emotions running high, on just about everything- (like on steroids)- you can apply the prowess that you have to any given situation by calling on your arsenal of tools.

Live vicariously at first. Because that's what imagination doe's -it pictures it. Then it seeks to transform you by taking note of the possibilities.

Some folks do this as a natural habit. Some will have to learn it as a skill. No one is perfect, no matter how spiritual or close to God that we

TRANSFORMATIVE BELIEFS: COUNTERBALANCE

consciously become in our hearts and minds. In the end-it is our prowess that saves us. God has put that mechanism into every living human being. Even some of the animals have it.

You should be actively involved in your evolution- by applying the filters and screeners.

We will experience a revolution when all thoughts are one and the same. And when they seek to go back to their original source-which is as a spark or seed. A seed that is tucked deep inside of you and protected-ready to pass on in piecemeal and parts to the next generation.

Thoughts of a wise person; is to know that everything originates along the spectrum and is developed between the heart (feeling) and brain (active screeners and filters).

This knowledge has great implication. You will have "cause and effect" along the spectrum even when you are void of knowledge. Brain- power, catches waves that are already in the atmosphere. It flows through the wind and speaks to us softly. Each time we can "catch" an original thought it leads to growth. Anytime we can 'check' our emotions and feelings-that are automatic and unique to the situation, we can use what we have and know, to demonstrate our ability to conquer.

Ihsan Jones

I like living in the moment. But not until (after) I have thought about a situation- to therefore, give a measured response.

Will I make mistakes? Yes, of course.

Will I always get a chance to apply the filters correctly? It's not likely; but at least I will have a second chance.

[I can live and learn along the spectrum with heartfelt beats sounding in the background like drums that are humming as I stroke them.]

Anything that's out of sync will be noticed. But that's not necessarily a bad thing-that's just me-trying to get it right.

CHAPTER 4- PRAGMATIC PLACEMENT

Developing Wisdom: A Pragmatic Plan

Is wisdom required to develop an understanding of honing the senses? No. But wisdom can be a catalyst since it can be obtained as part of the process. Remember that virtual reality is role play. And wisdom is an acquisition of knowledge that has accumulated over time. To develop and hone the senses as nature requires that we should; we would have to demonstrate maturity. Being in tune with vibes doesn't necessarily make you smart. It's the non- verbal communication (body language) that makes up the path as well. Only you know what it is that's affecting you. Only you, can know your true responses. As stated before, you can mask it from others. But that is not the purpose of these exercises. Nor is it the purpose of using the tools. Asking yourself the hard questions of why it is you feel this way-is the first step. Then making the play world adapt -to you as the star. Play whatever role you feel you need to, to imagine that it is you as the central player. Developing a pragmatic plan for honing the senses through virtual reality involves re-adapting an unlearned skill by re-enactment. It's not complicated nor is it rocket science. It just takes a vivid imagination to fulfill your dreams. Once you have 'felt' the activity taking place, you have met the requirements. Now, you have unlearned the skill of displaying the automatic reflex of (jealousy) for example, each time you encounter a similar situation. You can take a more measured approach with a pragmatic plan. Does that mean that you are required to imagine about everything? My answer is yes, if it is something that you truly want. Successful people that repeat these exercises can become skilled at adapting behavior. It is the actual episodes of having felt what it is you imagined that made it genuine. Now it's up to you, afterwards to see if it's something you want to pursue, or if it's really, worthwhile. Checks and balances along the scale don't always happen suddenly or by suppressing

TRANSFORMATIVE BELIEFS: COUNTERBALANCE

behavior. You would have to replace the autonomous skills (initial reactions) with something that's learned-mainly through your values. As you grow and learn you will mature. Wisdom is self-applied learning. Basically, as you venture, you grow. No one can obtain wisdom for you. It is you developing and honing the senses until you are in control enough to say that your first and initial response dos not have to be your lasting impression.

Use the wheel to adapt your behavior. This is setting up a pragmatic plan for counterbalance exercises. Make use of intra-gleaning if you need some spiritual guidance-to clean house. You can be caught off guard if your armoir is not filled enough to off- set-erratic and unbridled behavior. Learn the adaptation skills and techniques. First, they would involve displacement-then replacement with "you" as the star of the scene. Second, you can give a measured and controlled response by acknowledging your first behavior. Remember that being honest is a crucial part of adapting and using the controls of where you would want to land on the wheel which is used as a tool to quickly change and alter behavior along the spectrum. You can be the one pulling the strings-over time, as you adapt. Remembering that the idea is to counter the response eliciting the behavior -is how you will eventually gain more control. It's not that the gut reaction is no longer there. Nor is it being clouded by you masking it enough to not necessarily be revealed. What you are doing is replacing values with the responses that can negatively affect and impact your emotions and feelings.

[Demonstration of wheel *(see back pages) -wheel regarding sentiments offset with a virtue]

We're fortunate to be able to see the atmospheric patterns and changes that occur over time as they relate to our biological rhythms. Having a wheel to turn as a handy tool that displays emotions versus virtues as counterintuitive measures- gives us the upper hand at solving many problems by learning behavior techniques of adaptation. We can swap out the good for the bad in many instances. Eventually, although each behavior is autonomous (meaning it occurs alone at the onset of whatever excites it), we also can see the patterns that we have over time to make a more sensible approach. Much of what we are doing is similar, to cause and effect situations that our reality presents. We are acting in the present (the moment of ignition or excitement of our senses), then we use our

TRANSFORMATIVE BELIEFS: COUNTERBALANCE

cognition to rebel against the instantaneous feedback or bio-rhythms. Intuitively, we can off-set, or counterbalance any feeling or emotion that we run across. We can do this over and over until it becomes synchronized. Then as a conductor of our own symphony, we will become the masters in control. Our heart strings can continue to be pulled, but over time, we will have matured enough to know that a measured response is sometimes better than acting in accord to how we would feel. You might not want someone to know that you are jealous or envious. Because it may be just a symptom. Inside, you would have felt it, but it doesn't have to always be displayed. The wheel is a reminder of what you can think about instead. And like the -mind bending and floating techniques that we sometimes use when we choose to use virtual reality for displacement (basically putting you as the star in the scene that you would want to navigate), using the wheel, is yet another tool. It is visual, and therefore introduces a tangible element into the equation to help you work towards adapting behavior. Anything repeated twice, gets registered on the brain. Imagine if it is done several times over a lengthy period whenever it is needed. Whenever our emotions are developing into sentiments that would take us backward instead of forward. We would want to always be progressing towards our goal. The goal is to swap out a negative instantaneous combustion reaction with one that is more measured so that in the moment of truth-your truth, when you are interacting with someone-you can't be caught off guard.

A lot of folks like using meditation-to concentrate on positive vibes- to synchronize behavior. This is also one of the techniques of intra-gleaning which is spiritual in nature and can affect the heart. The heart is giving the responses, but the brain is using control mechanisms such as screening to work as a filter. filter. Using the brains power to contemplate on the good (of something) rather than focusing on the bad elements that can steer you wrong. Along with the wheel, you can make use of meditation as one more tool in the armoire/chest.

CHAPTER 5- REPEATING SOULS

Making mistakes that can be altered over time with time proven techniques, is a way to understand that we are repeating souls. Repeating souls are- new souls with old behavior. History repeats a million times and ignites in the atmosphere. We capture those ignitions as pre-thought. Which is, cognitive thinking skills that are capable of picking up on synchronized feelings that we all have. There is nothing new under the sun because nature adapts according to circumstance. We can and will make our presence felt and known under given situations. The concept of everything repeating itself is demonstrated first in the atmosphere, then in our behavior. No matter what it is that we learn, its already been here as a remnant of the past. We can't discover anything that doesn't adapt. This is how we can learn from our abilities as star performers that are on an earthly mission. Everything repeats. I mentioned before about the concept of waste that's reconstituted. New growth is a pattern of adaptation. Our souls are on constant repeat. Repetitive behavior is synonymous with the wheel of counter intuitiveness and sphere of emotions. We will have the same feelings over and over, only our sentiments about things will change. That's why feelings will always be as a 'gut reaction' whether you display them or not. It is the first true and most accurate response. We are pure spirits that come and go. We don't get to change ourselves except as it relates to demonstrating our emotions. That is why we have angelic qualities just as our predecessors did as well as those commanded by God to look after us. Super powers means being super intuitive with prowess. We possess the ability to change our thoughts, minds, and actions in the blink of an eye. We are on repeat until we can evolve with maturity and possibly gain wisdom in the process. Insight is a part of wisdom, but it is limited to what it is that we are contemplating. We live, and we die, in victory or defeat. Our defect is from not having a pure heart- meaning that the consciousness, hasn't cleared

TRANSFORMATIVE BELIEFS: COUNTERBALANCE

itself, yet. There is no sin in raw emotion and feelings. These are our natural inclinations. How we sin, is to meet the expectations of our imperfections. Much of it is in retaliation directly related to how we develop.

Souls repeat because God has given us autonomy in our biological rhythms. We can all hear and see the same drumbeat, but it may be felt a different way. Its according to how we're strummed, what has affected us in our past and going forward into our future. Some folks want to believe that ALL future mistakes have been forgiven because we are on automatic pilot as repeating souls. But the soul's embers haven't settled yet even if the fires have been put out. That's why bland(ness) is an option for us and why sometimes, our sentiments are actually-turned off-or held at bay.

God can sleep too- as our soul's rest. The angels are awakened (for us), as our souls become riled. They would get less sleep, to carry out their duties, as they keep watchful eyes in varying shifts. What we think is a random occurrence really is not. We've been shape shifting all along. Transforming ourselves, and, reshaping into our beliefs. So, there is an existence of heaven and hell, but most of it is inside. The turmoil, the anguish-that's felt from the pressure of living and making mistakes. So, is there really something happening here on earth where we should be 'cracking the code' to our existence? It's the rivalry of the consciousness and soul. One is awake while the other is sleeping. But they both exist to give us our awareness. Heaven and hell are domains. They both exist to feed our cognitive abilities while the brain is held tightly in a pressure cooker. We can withstand anything as time allows. Even the ability to change our minds about ideas. Like time capsules-we rise and fall with each occasion we encounter. We would have to use our counter intuitive measures as survival tools. Much of what we can filter through the spectrum can literally hold us down. Like gravity, it is a force. That's why the angels are on duty because the notion of higher power is a gift. We haven't grasped the brevity, yet, of what our skills entail. Gravity works for and against us. We have- to be reminded of this cause and effect relationship. That's how we distinguish the difference between qualities-such as heaven and hell. Two factors that influence how we live. We give preferential treatment to that which we feed. We can't get rid of the notion that somehow some folks are doing better than us and therefore we should be jealous. Jealousy is not just a part of the hellish domain, jealousy can also be heaven sent. It's the cognitive awareness part-that lends the separation. How cognizant

TRANSFORMATIVE BELIEFS: COUNTERBALANCE

are you…that you're jealous? Do those feelings arise because you've missed out on something, or does someone have something that's better than you and you think that you should have it too? There are so many reasons for understanding the sphere in which you operate when it comes to jealousy. This can be true for most sentiments. You pick one(sentiment)-name it. And pull it out of a hat. Is it a random feeling? Does it appear to come out of the blue? For sure, (that feeling), is not made it. But it can be made out to be more than it is.

Souls on repeat are always listening. We're turned on and tuned in. Our synchronization clock is ticking like a time bomb trying to tell us; Is it really our nature to 'give in' to this thought -or pre-thought that's already exists and is now trying to take control? Prowess is summoned -as a counter tactic. Be aware that your prowess is necessary if you want to re-channel and refocus. Otherwise, you will be fighting with hells fury to stop the havoc that jealousy (or any other sentiment), can reap on the soul.

Just know that you are blessed. And yes, the angels do have to intervene sometimes. They become our helpers because we don't always know where our sentiments will lead us. Oftentimes, they can stray beyond our control if we let them get the best of us. If an angel intervenes, like the stroke of a pen-it can be wiped out. Peace is another domain that rests between the other two (heaven and hell). Also, bland; where something is turned off. Where, on the spectrum, would you find your peace? It all depends on how well you can manipulate those past -gut-feelings that can make you do crazy things. Peace can shape the world by changing attitudes. It's like switching arenas where we can be rewarded as we act according to our faith. Faith is built upon the principles that houses virtues, and it becomes clear that our values are meaningful as we apply them. This is what takes us to our highest standards- of living. We can't have life without some sort of discord. Without stoking up our feelings. But discord is not random. It happens as we experience it.

CHAPTER 6- RANDOMNESS

Are there things that we experience in life-out of our control? Randomness is a thought pattern that appears to be out of synchronization. There appears to be randomness in everything that we do. But are things truly random? Is it like the 'bland' part of the bandwidth on the spectrum-unexpected? Every now and then, and occasional- something will happen, unexpected that's out of the ordinary. Was this also part of a plan? Or is it just the way that things are lining up? If there ever was a plan-how could randomness explain it? This is something peculiar about being random, but it is not at all odd.

For something to truly be random, we should not be able to predict it. On the spectrum of cognitive synergies that develop between our hearts and our brains, which in turn arouses our sentiments; there is a part along the spectrum where we cannot drum or stir up any of thoughts or feelings.

Nor, can we make any predictions. Even our pre-play as a subset of our prescript, is set, to some extent. We can dream exactly how we would want to feel, if our consciousness lets us. Similar, to the odor of any aroma – a smell cannot be predicted simply by looking at its package. To predict the aroma, you would have to become familiar with the scent, over time, once the source has been examined. So, predictability and randomness do not appear to coincide, but they can coexist. We should be able to tell, over time exactly what some of the options could be based on comparisons to the source. We would need to use our reference tools such as pre-screening. Aside from our gut or initial reaction (as to whether we like it or not)- an aroma can be traced back to its source and we will handle it (the situation) based on our categorization. We can re-train our brains to give certain responses regardless of the scent. Over time, the thought of perfume can be imagined. But so, can other smells. We even can add scenery that pleases our senses. Once we have had the experience, the randomness, (or strangeness) of the effects will wear off. Then we would have the ability to predict an aroma. Our senses respond accordingly to the randomness of the scent and make preparation to categorize then as either good, bad, or neutral. Your mood can change in an instant based on the randomness of a smell.

What else is there about randomness besides the fact that it means that something is beyond our control? Remember, with randomness, you can't make compromises. It is what it is-just like the smell. Randomness does not control our ideas or thinking. Nor does it mean that it's gone awry. The importance of randomness is that-to control our senses when we come across 'different' and or unexpected experiences, we would have to regroup them in such a way as to manage control.

We should remember that everything exists as pre-thought. And pre-thinking- is a part of our makeup and that we can't randomly just make up things. Everything has a category and must coincide with something. Our consciousness streams are capturing pre-thoughts to literally dispose of them and move them around. The brains power is, 'turned on,' all the time; even when the body is resting. This is also what we must know about the presentations that exist in the world. They are always there but are being filtered according to their presentation. The rest is being done by our hearts, according to how we feel. Then the brain receives these signals, to screen them further based on what we know about our present and past.

Subconsciously, our senses are pre-conclusions that are drawn from our experiences. And if we haven't experienced something yet-that's when we can view it as random. Because we haven't run across a category from which to choose.

As you can see-randomness is not truly random-because the thoughts that exist in our head are figuring out ways to process what we can't see and what's going on behind the scenes. Like the smell, no matter what we think about something, as we try to figure it out-the end result, is to process a decision based on the options. Decision making is what we might have control over- but- definitely, not the selections. Randomness is preselected memories that are directly tied to our fate. Their destination will be based on how effectively, we use the tools.

On a larger scale, the world operates truly on the randomness of pre-inclined destinations. There are inclinations given, that the world is headed in a certain direction. But that doesn't preclude any thought process-because we still would need to sort things out. This takes us back to the concept of "the greater good". Much sacrifice is made in the name of the greater good- or, doing what's necessary, regardless of the sacrifice or cost.

TRANSFORMATIVE BELIEFS: COUNTERBALANCE

But who's greater good would that be? Those who are deciding the fate? As people, we can be manipulated. But the mechanism that controls us (holds us down -literally) is our own way of thinking. We can be held captive-like in a jail cell, pretending to be free. This is because those prepatterns of inclination originating from the source, can include, mind control. Shouldn't we be worried about whose thoughts are controlling us- other than God? This is not random. This is by design, because we should always have to think about the source. Any source or pattern that preexists, it is not chosen randomly- by God. The Source, or Pattern, is the reason that we question things in the first place. It is the options that are presented according to our existence. There is acting on stage-there is awareness, and there are predetermined 'acts', according to Gods plan. So, the randomness that we experience is predestined by God. It is the encounters and challenges that we have, with everything, that pre-shapes, our soul.

When you think of randomness, go back to natures calling and it becomes a consciousness stream that's tuned in to our awareness based on what category something fits it, or more-so, with our familiarity.

As we give thought to randomness…we should just know that things exist, because they are shaping up to set us off on a course of pre-destined actions. You will act according to how you feel. Your feelings are deeply tied to your sentiments.

Randomness can be related to the synergies along the spectrum. You might not know how you're going to feel about something until it actually 'hits', you-when you will have given your gut response. Even if you can see the package-like the scent-you can't always predict the smell. People and situations will have direct effect on you, and it will be up to you to adjust your senses accordingly.

Understanding randomness is important because- if we can know the patterns of 'how' we arrive at things (making decisions, based on our sentiments), then we can better control them. Improvising through virtual reality may be adventurist; but is also allows us a unique way to escape so that the end result; is having better control over our emotions; senses and feelings.

"If I have lived it before (even in my mind), then I have experienced it. Then, if I want to somehow, put those actions in motion-and experience it in real life, then I could set on a path to make it happen."

TRANSFORMATIVE BELIEFS: COUNTERBALANCE

That's why virtual reality is a viable option when dealing with the 'selection' or options of randomness. You can use it as a tool to sharpen your instincts-in regards, to how you would react.

It's like learning a new language in another form of communication. Only you are doing it (the virtual reality), with yourself. Pre-thoughts have a way of presenting as ideas. But those pre-thoughts will only manifest through actions, if you have the desire to live them out. A lot of times we are satisfied with just having the experience in our minds. The reason for that is because some thoughts-should never escape. They should stay locked up until the bittersweet aroma has subsided and mellowed out. Then a decision can be made as to whether, or not this virtual reality world-should in fact-become real.

The brains interaction with pre-thought is to question its relationship to its source. The source is the sentiment it's tied to, e.g., "am I jealous?". The idea that's spun around the sentiment in your head has, to be imaged or presented, then put together. Precisely where the information is coming from may not ever be known, but you will know that information over time as patterns develope. "Do I always get jealous when presented with similar circumstances? Or, is this just an isolated incident based on what's happening now?" Timing becomes everything, in regards, to randomness. There might even be pre-conditions for our preclusions, But, most, will never happen is we don't act on it. Much of our pre-thought presents as mirror images of what we would want to happen. How things will actually-turn out, is another story. Therefore, as pre-conclusions, there is never a guarantee from the onset which scenario (based on our experience with randomness) will be the selection, until we have made up in our minds, and through conditioning, what it is we would want to world to see. Knowing about this (how you could react) ahead of time, can save us from a lot of situations. Use the tools. The spectrum provides many opportunities for honing and fine tuning the scale based on virtues and values.

Your initial or gut reaction may be a surprise. Like randomness, you can't predict how something will affect you. There are so many ingredients that go into the presentations (of randomness). That is why we would have to rely on the filtering and screening processes to essentially give us a 'second chance".

TRANSFORMATIVE BELIEFS: COUNTERBALANCE

You can't hide 'gut reaction", you can only mask it because you can't hide it-from yourself. You can play along and pretend that you didn't 'feel' a certain way. But if you are venturing into the negativity that our senses can sometimes take us- that's when we must reassess. Vicariously place yourself into a position where you would not be jealous (through virtual reality), make yourself feel as if you too have experienced this "thing" so that you won't be jealous. Use the 'man in the mirror' concept to call upon your virtues instead of your negativity.

The best way to forgive someone (even if they have done nothing more than to make you feel a certain way), is to vicariously, and infamously make the preparations (in our thoughts), to live as you think they do-and walk in their shoes which you will have custom fit-to your own.

This is the remedy that adjusts the scale. Our emotions will flare-up, randomly, in response to our perceptions. We also would have the ability to rescale, reshape, and glamorize the situation. It would be like, wearing accessories.

Human beings are so intimately tied to how we would feel that it affects others. God allows random access as pre-shaping and pre-conditioning.

We must readjust ourselves accordingly. It is our thoughts about a certain subject that could determine the conclusion.

We can improve ourselves based on the tools. The more virtuous qualities we can exhibit-the more we will have to draw upon. There is nothing like -using our acting skills (vicariously) to reshape them.

Reshaping our pre-conditions takes a concerted effort. We can use our consciousness stream as recall. Hopefully, we have filtered enough to not always allow negative responses unless we feel it is warranted. You can re-set the design of the mechanism but not the source. The source is what we all are made of. No one is capable of duplicating, deleting, or erasing, what God has ordained, which is our natural ability to react and respond based on the scale of the spectrum. We can be altered. This is also what we are doing with our attempts at reshaping how we should feel and react at any given time. How we should feel is directly connected to our values and virtues. We can be self-made, as we make our adjustments. Virtues are learned over time, and throughout history, no one has been able to form an interaction in society, without first, having been shaped and influenced.

TRANSFORMATIVE BELIEFS: COUNTERBALANCE

As group thinkers (because we are born into groups of people that look after us), we will have group thoughts that represents preset behaviors as responses to what we know. But everyone will be different as to how something affects them. What makes me jealous may not make another person jealous or feel the same. Our unique set of sentiments become our qualities; yet, these are what we all have in common. We might not always act and feel the same way, but we can share the same sentiments. Maybe not all at once. But this uniqueness in our qualities represents our 'humanity'. And to remedy and adjust the scales, we must look further and deeper inside -to pick and choose, based on our values.

Ihsan Jones

-INTERIM-

Have you had your Super Visit?

I've had several. My latest one was at the funeral home.

At the Funeral Home...

※ ※ ※

I'd arrived, well, sort of late. It was only after driving all day and for several more hours that I'd come to realize, that we might not make it. I was riding in the car with my youngest daughter and her two children. The kids had been patient all day considering the long trip. We had to travel the interstate to reach our destination. Traffic was slow at times because of the burning fires that had been reported on the news. You

TRANSFORMATIVE BELIEFS: COUNTERBALANCE

could still smell their embers plus see the devastation of the land and homes that the fire had destroyed. We had left on that trip knowing that we were taking a chance. To travel through the hills and mountains and get stuck-was a real possibility. But we both saw past that, my daughter and, I.

I could tell by the decision we made; which was to take off without regards to what might be happening on the road. We both had hoped the road would be clear of course-but just in case we had charted an alternate route. This route would seem cumbersome at times because it meant waiting through traffic and experiencing sharp inclines that were close to the ridges of the fire. The fires had not yet been contained and we knew it. But we also knew that the path forward required our immediate attention.

My sister had passed away, and I was in a desperate state to try and see her before we could lay her to rest. I had to travel the furthest it seems since my other siblings lived there, locally and I had to travel from out of state. Nevertheless, time was passing and at times traffic seemed like it was at a crawl. Aside from me weeping (silently) most of the way- I had no time to think about the immediate danger. If the route wasn't going to be safe, then we would find out. We also could turn around if we had to. But I so desperately needed to get there so we trekked on. Even flying would have been cumbersome with the last- minute costs of purchasing tickets. So, we drove.

The closer we got to the hills where the devastating fire had already killed lots of folks who had been trapped in their homes or had no means of escape- and even though we were going around-so I thought, it seemed that this pre-destination had been chosen. I was no longer joy riding-even though sad from my sister's situation because traveling through those burnt out hills reminded me, in general, of people's struggle. We take a lot of things for granted; our health, our wealth, and our happiness. I saw this most while traveling through the hills. We view it in light, of things that are tangible. But the things that should matter the most-we can't see (e.g. the forest because of the trees). The true beauty lies within your inner circle and we sometimes take that for granted. Because of the burnt trees I could actually "feel", death, even before I got to the funeral home.

But once we arrived (almost at the very last minute before the viewing would be over), my feelings were overwhelming again and begun to get the best of me. I had flooded with tears already (inside) while traveling along

TRANSFORMATIVE BELIEFS: COUNTERBALANCE

the road. I also had said a silent prayer for those victims of the wildfire. But at the funeral home I could see my family again and although sad-still be happy. I was happy that everyone was together but not happy about the circumstance under which we were all drawn together. Emotions were high-tears were overwrought, and I felt imprisoned by the fact that such a small place could be holding the spirit (and actual body) of my sister who was once lively and bubbly. Her infectious smile was tantamount to her spirit and I could only pray that she was at peace. While standing there in her presence, it felt like she was.

I hadn't paid too much- close attention to the detail of the funeral home before now. I had been here before, to visit a loved one who had also passed. The lighting was bright, people were all over the place, in every room. We all were there to say our goodbyes before the actual funeral which would be held in a couple of days.

There had been chatter about those who were sick in the family, and how much "strangeness" everyone was experiencing at this time-the time of the California wildfires. I felt it too. But mostly, I felt the loss of my dearly departed sister whom I loved so much. She was two years younger than me, so we were close.

Ihsan Jones

My eyes welled up as I stood there practically in a trance because everything seemed surreal and I was secretly wishing that it could all go away. That maybe, I could wake up from a dream and everything would go back to normal. But is wasn't a dream-it was real.

At one point while standing in the room glancing at her, there seemed a need to get the funeral director's attention. So, I rushed from the room to get the help.

As I was walking, a strange thing happened. I saw someone walking fast paced across a room, so I approached it. To my surprise, no one was there. One side of the room was lit bright and I could see upon further examination that it was a display room for the things they would sell like urns, caskets, etc. the other side of the room was dark, but it was were the form had walked briskly too that I had tried to catch up to. I could feel the presence of something summoning me to that dark side and since I felt uncomfortable, I darted out. I turned to the people standing close by and asked them where the person had gone that walked across that room. Their responses were, that the attendant was in the room with them and they didn't see anybody in the room I had just come out of. So, I had been

TRANSFORMATIVE BELIEFS: COUNTERBALANCE

chasing a shadow it seemed-but the shadow had summoned me to come in there. The attendant immediately followed me afterwards as I explained the situation. He was jovial, but attentive. With the smile on his face, I couldn't help but think that maybe he knew something about -my previous experience. I let it go, at the time. Mentioned it to my children later- on. And have decided to share that experience in this book. The reason is twofold. One, is because of my undying love for my sister and the memories I want to hold onto of her. And the second reason is because I have always been prone to visits -from those that have either died or passed on.

The spirit that was in that room had summoned me. Why? I don't know. I don't even have an inkling of who it might be.

But the conclusion, is that we do have what are called super visits. They can be in the form of angels that can help us or from those who want you to feel their presence and/or, can be passing on a message. Super visits for myself, happen frequently. I can recall in great, detail, each time such an occurrence has happened.

What I have come to know about super visits is that, the strangeness of them will stick with you. It will be in your gut feeling as to who and what the circumstances might be surrounding the reason for them visiting you. They could be acting as a hero (your savior) in the middle of a crisis or could be bringing you a message that's profound in consequence.

I have learned to not question the presence of an entity as to whether it's friend or foe. But what I have learned to do, is to channel that energy, which is the underlying spirit from it-wishing that it the best of luck and that is it is bringing me hope.

We are all aligned with our destiny. We cannot only fathom the joy and richness that God brings to us through agents as messengers. But should contemplate the learning aspects of it as well. We grow in spirit ourselves, when we can recognize that other's spirits, will remain. On the spectrum- of things. That is also where we can find the peace.

ABOUT THE SUPER VISITS…

Super visits are spiritual lessons and words from God that can only transform us when they reach our consciousness, and when we recognize them. It is a message intended just for you as instruction and guidance and that shadows your behavior on earth.

Super visits can be done in several ways-but mostly, they begin with revelation.

First, you must be presented with a situation. Then, a remedy is revealed (given to you in the form of context or dialogue). You may not be consciously aware-or recognize the burden of carrying that now consciously made decision to carry the "heavy" load. It can be very 'heavy', although in some respects, a weight will have been lifted, once you've gotten the clearer message of what it was all about or what it is that you need to do. Lifting burdens requires an episode that's purely conscious driven and heartfelt.

God delivers those that are in crisis, but also when we're not in crisis. It takes an episode to be created first before we can experience it. Avoidance is done by happenstance and only after knowing. That's why remaining silent, or on the sidelines, once you receive those messages of intervention- is unavoidable. You should have to, at the very least, acknowledge it and recognize it as coming from-an intervention.

Ihsan Jones

God has enough subordinates to coordinate not having to intervene unless it is absolutely, necessary and required. So, if you would venture to say that God is not sleeping. I would say that God can be quiet and is not always loud. Therefore, God can get some rest knowing that we have been given the tools for our protection. Everything is competent based-meaning, that we must learn.

We must learn our lessons according to how we feel.

We can feel one way or another about a situation, and since God has armored us with the wherewithal to hold fast and steady (even under pressure) and stand up for our truths-we must live with the consequences of our actions every day. This is, why, we can also be caught up in others vicious cycles. Everything we do will not be hunky dory-nor will they be that way when they come to past. Living as we are, for now, requires active engagement.

Some of the tools that we learn about through living, can be the same tools that ostracize. For example, love, can begin as love (while we are enamored with it affectionately), then, turn into hate.

Why?

TRANSFORMATIVE BELIEFS: COUNTERBALANCE

Because it's a spectrum. A spectrum of living and learning from our past. That spectrum can be diabolical too, because wires can get crossed, misfires can happen-and we can become over- zealous in our way of thinking about a lot of things. To put things into perspective, we would have to understand the nature of the requirements that God has given us. They are a pre-set of instructions tapped into our domain. Our domain is our brain that originates from the sentiments nursed and encouraged from our hearts.

Here are the feelings we are supposed to exhibit in a moment of crisis or otherwise:

They can be; hate, love, envy, misery, respect, disrespect, etc., etc.

These will not be in any- particular, order. They rest on a scale. A scale by which we can have- random access. And since we have random access to our feelings-we can also exhibit control.

EMOTIONS RUN HIGH

Synergies- Why we feel them and what they are?

Because the spectrum has a set of "hard and fast' rules that are based on our sentiments. We can emit cross fields of energy projection that can flow inwardly as well as outwardly. This is called something like radiation that has penetrated until it has found its position.

Like a prize possession-it settles in on the sentiment that's been stoked, before it moves along its path.

We can halt it by-garnering and corralling the strangeness of the synergies that's affecting us.

And although the path, is all too familiar (remains constant)- we don't know how we'll be affected.

We respond with: How I react? vs How should I react? These two are mutually exclusive. We can see that one is a spirit that has been invoked or strummed up, while the other is being summoned (by us) and being called in to save us. Both are underlying spirits coinciding with the spectrum. This can explain ALL behaviors and why they deeply affect us. We are trying to rescue and save ourselves, and when we don't or can't, some other entity known as angels can intervene. We are synergies emitting trust and

TRANSFORMATIVE BELIEFS: COUNTERBALANCE

trustworthiness along with mistrust and unworthiness, as our true source. And the preclusions, as endings, will have different scenarios. That is what happens. And this (the source) precludes our existence and is an explanation as to why we all have the unique qualities coming from our individual source (called the spectrum). It was preprogrammed and pre-wired, as part of our existence.

CHAPTER 7- ALL THE THINGS THAT MATTER

The Un-meaningfulness of Things

Imagine not knowing or understanding much- about anything. This still doesn't mean we will not have a response. It means that the mechanism for responding is obscured through displacement. We must first, be able to filter what we have learned about things-to sort them out. Displacement of sentiments is different. Because when sentiments become displaced (such as through 'lack of association', lack of understanding-or simply confusion, we tend to be engaging in what is called 'cross wires'. The crossed wires can lead to confusion with displaced souls. But- EVERYTHING is meaningful. It just means it hasn't had its right association. Blandness is not directly tied to unmeaningful. Bland is a holding state. And like Peace-which can be used as a metaphor, so can blandness. The spectrum releases the blandness in the form of unrisen eclectic response. We have elected not to respond based on what we don't know. If we don't know the details of something or don't have a general reference as a starting point-then the confusion results as bland-or nothing that is stoked. Except, maybe only curiosity. But curiosity isn't a sentiment. It is a part of our prowess. It is the king and queen of what originates in our bodies that's called 'lost'. Not, loss as in deaf dumb or blind, but lost as in-simply not having a reference or knowledge point, to make the association. It is being "kid" like, in a sense. Which is fresh and new. So, the unmeaningful-ness of things does not touch us in respects to anything that we have 'actually' lost. But it does touch us in the way of what we haven't 'gained'. You can have this type of confusion along the scale of the spectrum. It can result in 'mixed' feelings about something or 'no' feelings at all. You would have to use the filtering mechanism of the brain to churn the wheels to better classify what it is you have been exposed to, to better understand the pinnacle you have reached. It's like a person standing still when they should run. Or, someone that didn't understand the question that was asked which results in a facial expression of deer in headlights.

A "weighted" response can only be measured with time. It takes time to seal in the warning signals that control the mechanism. The more you learn, the more you know. The more you develop and seek out the learning, then you have greater chances of honing that information. You want to be sure it can be used in a category as a reference point so that the "dot of origin" logs it in. The wheel will provide us the tools. We can spin ourselves out of control or we can "kneel" in prayer- and ask God to help us via the Angels. We also, can just-let things be- until…in our minds…they become…sorted out.

THE CONCEPT OF NOTHINGNESS

Nothing ventured, nothing gained. Why is this the way we develop? Why is it, that God has chosen for us, this form of a ruse? Is it because that is a part of the living cycle? At first, we know nothing. Then as we grow-we develop. So… does things like learning about concepts result in our maturity?

They can, once we have learned their proper perspective?

What is there about "nothing" that stands out?

It's because "nothingness" is a concept, and not our actual reality. There is no such thing as something 'not' being there-it is simply missing. Confused? Let me explain this concept further…

The "dot of origin" is a concept. We can use it to figuratively explain how something (that we can't seem to touch or feel) is there. Let alone, not being able to see it. But in all fairness to this over used conceptualized way of saying that 'something, or either 'nothing- is there…then we must look at the scale of latitude that occurs among the spectrum. Let's see…there is blandness, peaceful, resting, and, also something called 'nil'. Nil is akin to none. Which would also be another way of saying that something isn't there.

The dot of origin is the originality that God has put into us. It is the ingenuity and creativity of life. There can never be 'nothing' but what there is…is something, that hasn't been developed or created…yet.

Ihsan Jones

If you don't get it- think about the way that something is either made or discovered. It never comes out of thin air. It is usually, and generally…unmasked. Basically, it's dug up from something that's already there or from two or more things that can be fused. And the confusion comes from the fact that we haven't developed it yet. So, is there nothing? Or, is there something, that's waiting to be discovered? Clearly, it would take the dot of origin to sort this one out. The concept of nothing, then, has- to be 'dug up' and made into something first-before it can be recognized. This is the what happens on the scale and how sentiments become escalated and organized. It is because they were always there-they needed to be stoked or strummed so we could recognize their existence. Ignition goes hand in hand with the concept of "nothingness'. First, there needs to be a spark…then a flare…and you know what happens after that? The situation is either spun out of or into our control. Take note that the scale of counterbalance helps us realize any misplaced categories.

TRANSFORMATIVE BELIEFS: COUNTERBALANCE

THE STRUCTURE OF IMBALANCE

Finding the right balance to something is a plus. But we can't always get things right. There should have to be an opposite or counter to any argument, otherwise we could never flex our muscles to grow. Growth is the proper concept that helps us understand how effective the tools that we choose can be. Remember, when there is nothingness, that something -had to be "dug up" to unmask it, and then use it to fuse or formulate into something either original or duplicated.

Something, means Useful and Nothing, means-not having discovered it yet.

But it is clear, that ALL is there. We just can't see it. It starts as a pre-thought and precondition then develops further as we muster our 'feelings" towards it and try to understand. ALL things originate this way, whether they are conceptual, virtual, or, as we say…real. The purpose is to master our feelings and have them under control, not to hide who we really are as a person, but to be able to not inflict the harm that we can be prone to do when we make mistakes.

If the Angels can make mistakes working on God's behalf, then clearly, we are prone to do them. That's because we haven't yet mastered the concepts. And I suspect it will be our life long duty to try. What else do we have to do here on earth? Why is it, that we are 'really' living?

If you can 'seek' to control your own state of being-then maybe you also can help others. It's what we as 'human- being's' can do. It's what we do 'in fact' get right. Not from lack of trying-but from trying too hard. All we would need to do, is to understand the balance along the scales and accept the fact that the dot of origin (that brings and stirs our emotions), brings us tools right along with it, which are counter intuitive measures that can help us. What separates us as far as the 'weightiness' in which we would use the tools- is counterbalance. To counter something is to bring it back into alignment with where we think it ought to be. So, our alignment with "displacement" for example, is truly random until we can grasp it later. Using all the tools at our disposal: our virtues, values, and prayerful concepts like using

TRANSFORMATIVE BELIEFS: COUNTERBALANCE

the head-weights (ultra-gleaning, intra-gleaning, etc.) to discover who and what we are, or at least who we can become by using our Prowess. All of this goes into creating the structure of imbalance that we see along the scales.

Finding Peace-might be when we no longer should have to think about it. But it wouldn't mean that the structure (of imbalance) no longer exists. It should mean that things like bland and peace are only temporary- and that ALL things would be Possible as we arrange and engage with them along the scale of the spectrum. Most of our thoughts that are drummed up by emotions can be filtered-by using displacement in the form of virtual reality as a viable option, since it can replace whatever it is that we think we have lost and/or hoping for.

Ihsan Jones

CONCLUSION

COUNTER-BALANCE

There is a resistance movement that we have within us that can be viewed as a gift. It is our unique reference source that indicates how we should feel in our interactions. It included fields of energy like Destiny, Sin, Randomness. All of which are preclusions that act as if they are the rites to our souls.

The resistors are channeled energy that flows between the heart and brain, to shield the source of the mechanics that are stirred and strummed up. They represent cyclical imbalance in our lives as they fluctuate. It would take counter intuitive measures as well as our prowess, these are what makes up the body's constraints.

We can control that which we 'feel' only after coming into contact, with our initial or first reaction. This is our inner most feeling and "gut" response to outer stimulus.

Counter balance is a way to, not only-field the energy from the effects of the emotions, but also offers a plan of self-defense that counters the "ill" effects of our behavior based on experience. It moves along the spectrum until it registers the exact emotive that we've felt (before) in similar situations. Then, by distribution of what is familiar, or already known, we register the sentiment (after having dispensed with the initial one which gave us the shock affect) by basically, sorting it out. We tend to work through it as we pick and choose another response. This is known as displacement. We would need to displace the sentiment by association first, before we can make it a true representation of how we would want to feel, or more importantly, how we could give an alternative reaction to our 'first reaction'.

It is a gift that we can offer a different response so that the first response-doesn't appear to be -our lasting impression.

Are we acting? No, not really. Based on our experience of what we know that comes directly from how our values would influence us-is a better way to come to terms with having to replay, many of our scenes.

TRANSFORMATIVE BELIEFS: COUNTERBALANCE

The wheel in the diagram, provides a good representation of some of the things we might have to sort out.

The Wheel of Counter Balance *(see back pages)

The hearts synergies are in the middle.

Lines are reverberating and penetrating the fields, but also dispersed across the shields to the areas of counter intuitive measures

On one side there are fields of endearment of things that we are enamored with such as -honor, equality, love, honor, respect, decency. These tend to lie more towards the top. And at the bottom on the other side, are the paths that sentiments take-they can be estrangement, isolation, loneliness.

Use the wheel according to your value system. They are things that we have stored in our chest, locked in our hearts, but that can be drawn out as we need them.

Ihsan Jones

DISPLACEMENT/REPLACEMENT/VIRTUAL SOULS

Displacement is transforming our outer bodies to into realism
*Based on adjusting the scales

Replacement is replacing the negative thoughts with values that regenerate as new ideas

Virtual Souls-is to live as though nothing has changed (except, you as a person) having realigned to a better transformation

People can see the outer you. They can't see the inner you. As the scales adjust through displacement/ replacement- our virtual reality wheel spins and continues the adjustment. This would be our adjudication - which is to ask God to forgive, once we've outgrown -what it is, we use to do.

We are on auto pilot to self-heal, self-correct and reconstruct.
All of these, capabilities are built in us.
But it always suffices to say-that God is in full control and command of whatever it is that we can do-Not Us...
Because God has made the mechanism.

TRANSFORMATIVE BELIEFS: COUNTERBALANCE

* * *

END

This is the Start of the Drawings and Graphs contained in the Back Pages for reference with the text.

*Use them as guides to help you understand the inner cycles of the spectrum.

-List of virtues-

Honor, integrity, loyalty, decency, grace, goodness, courage, bravery, compassion, respect, dignity… this list goes on and on.

-List of values-

Commitment, acceptance, cooperation, attendance, attentive, consistency, charitable, giving, achievement, accountability, benevolence…this list crosses over into the virtues.

*Reference the drawings and depictions of the Counter intuitive tools such as the Wheel of Counterbalance, Dot of Remembrance and the Spectrum. There are counter measures to be used as productive tools -that treasure our body, mind, and spirit- so ultimately, we can gain inspiration through intra and ultra-gleaning- which is- prayer, meditation, and self-reflection.

TRANSFORMATIVE BELIEFS: COUNTERBALANCE

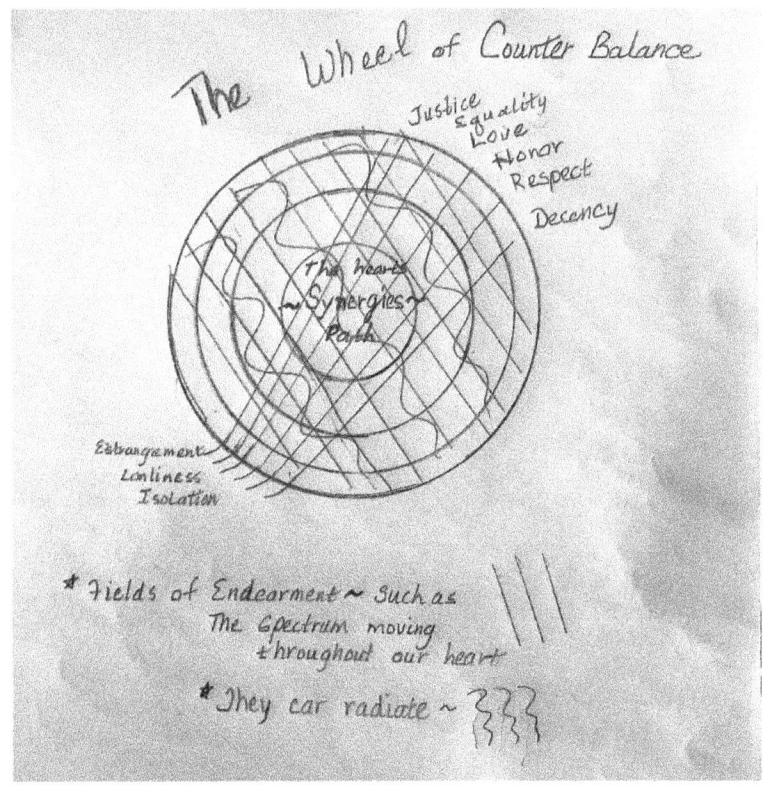

Ihsan Jones

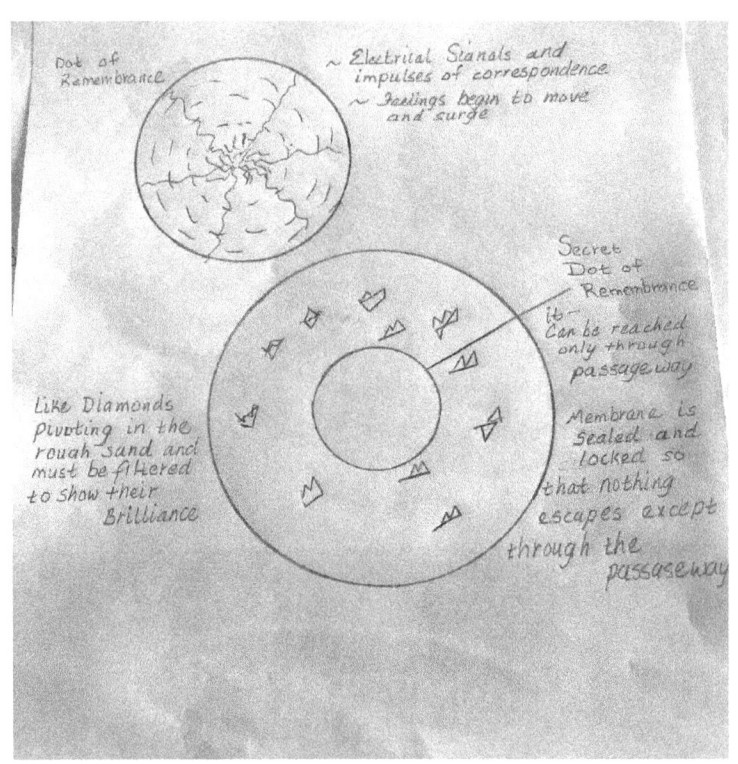

TRANSFORMATIVE BELIEFS: COUNTERBALANCE

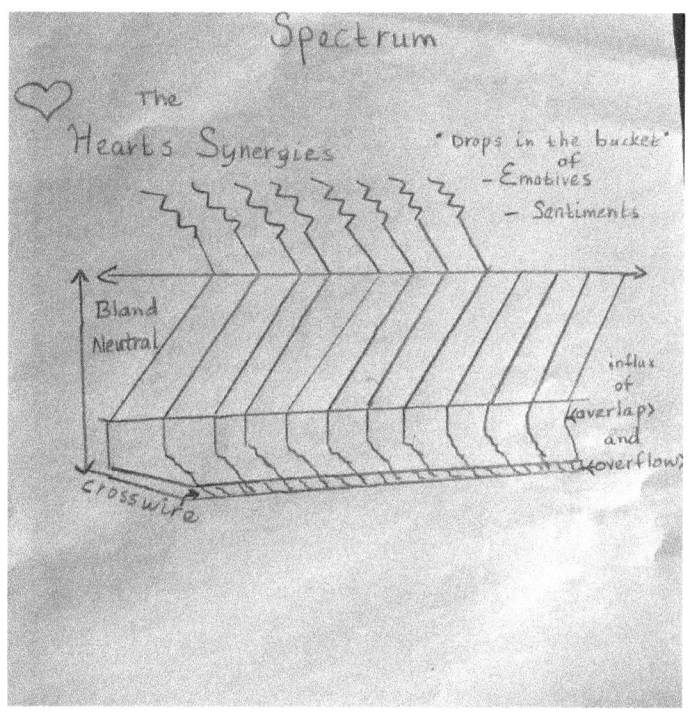

Ihsan Jones

www.ingramcontent.com/pod-product-compliance
Lightning Source LLC
LaVergne TN
LVHW041546070426
835507LV00011B/953